BEYOND THE BOX

EXPAND YOUR BLUES/ROCK GUITAR SOLOING

BY BUZZ FEITEN

Recording Credits:
Guitar: Buzz Feiten
Drums: Jason Smith
B-3: J.T. Thomas
Bass: Jorgen Carlson, Bass

Cover artwork by Levin Pfeufer
Photograph courtesy of Aleksandra Sever (www.aleksandrasever.com)

Cherry Lane Music Company
Educational Director/Project Supervisor: Susan Poliniak
Director of Publications: Mark Phillips
Publications Coordinator: Rebecca Skidmore

ISBN: 978-1-60378-175-6

Visit our website at www.cherrylaneprint.com

CONTENTS

INTRODUCTION

The recording that made me decide to become a guitar player was the John Mayall and the Bluesbreakers *"Beano"* album, featuring a young, unknown guitarist named Eric Clapton. That record just blew me away, as it did many of us who are old enough to remember it. It started me off in pursuit of the blues. I grabbed every recording I could find of artists such as B.B. King, Muddy Waters, Albert King, Howlin' Wolf, and many others. I became obsessed with learning blues riffs, licks, and styles, and when I was 19 years old, I joined the Butterfield Blues Band.

Now, I've worked 40 plus years as a professional guitarist, and at one point many years ago I became very dissatisfied with my soloing. I hit a wall, and it seemed that no matter what I tried, I just wasn't happy with my solos. They sounded very ordinary, with a lot of blues clichés and tired phrases that everybody else was playing. That's when I decided to stop thinking like a guitar player and start thinking like a sax or piano player. They are not limited by fret position, and their solos sound much more interesting to me. Instead of abandoning the blues, I decided to expand that style and add a whole new dimension to it, using the scales, arpeggios, intervals, and phrasing that I had absorbed over the years from the great musicians with whom I had been privileged to work.

The purpose of this book is to share that process of evolution and to provide other guitarists with the tricks and techniques I have learned over the years that have given me so much more freedom, joy, and satisfaction as a guitar player.

In addition, at the end of this book, I have included three examples from its companion book, *Exercises and Warm-Ups for the Blues/Rock Guitarist*. The exercises in that volume were written to help you to improve your technique and overcome the natural tendency to become complacent in your practicing and soloing.

Note: Track 1 contains tuning pitches.

ABOUT THE AUTHOR

Buzz Feiten started his professional career, while still in his teens, with an invitation to join the Paul Butterfield Blues Band. During his first night with the band, he jammed (on bass) in New York City with Butterfield, Al Kooper, B.B. King, and Jimi Hendrix. He was also with the Butterfield band when they played Woodstock. Buzz's natural gifts as a rhythm guitar player and as a passionate and melodic soloist have led him to record and perform with the likes of Stevie Wonder, Aretha Franklin, the Rascals, Gregg Allman, Bob Dylan, Rickie Lee Jones, Dave Sanborn, and Dave Weckl. He is also the inventor of the Buzz Feiten Tuning System.

The Buzz Feiten Model guitar is now available. To order Buzz's CDs, and for ordering information regarding the Buzz Feiten Model guitar, please visit www.buzzfeitenguitars.com, or email a request to buzz.feiten@yahoo.com.

Thanks for your support!

ACKNOWLEDGMENTS

I would like to give my deepest thanks to John Stix, Rebecca Skidmore, Susan Poliniak, and all the talented people who have supported me with encouragement and enthusiasm from the beginning.

THE SOLOIST AS STORYTELLER

As every writer knows, there are three basic parts to a story: the beginning, the middle, and the ending. The same concept applies to soloing on the guitar: Every great guitar solo has a beginning, a middle (or *development*), and an ending.

There are specific techniques for the visualization and creation of a solo. The first thing to consider is the concept or idea for the solo. I call it the "feeling tone" of a solo. It's the feeling that is inspired by the song, and it can be joyful, sad, playful, aggressive, or any of the other emotions of which we are capable.

The second thing is to visualize the solo—its structure and its curve (i.e., how and where the solo peaks in intensity).

The third is to apply your musical technique or "vocabulary" to the song. There are specific techniques that make up this soloist's "toolbox" of musical ideas. The better and wider your vocabulary, the more effortless and satisfying it should be to solo. Some of these techniques are available in the companion book/CD, *Warm-Ups and Exercises for the Blues/Rock Guitarist*, and some examples from that book are included in this volume. *Warm-Ups and Exercises* is a study method for improving your soloing, with exercises on scales, arpeggios, and intervals, along with basic technique instruction that can help to improve your speed, finger independence, phrasing, and overall command of the instrument. All of these techniques are learned, practiced, and refined over a lifetime.

THE STORY, PART I
The Beginning/Opening Statement

"Buzz's Blues"

Listen to "Buzz's Blues" on your CD. Can you hear how the opening phrase is an invitation? It's short and simple. Depending on the song, the opening phrase can be tender, mysterious, passionate, aggressive, etc. This is where you establish the feeling tone and harmonic center of the solo. It is the most important part of the solo, because it suggests the direction of the story and establishes a harmonic "home base" to which you will later return. The details of what happens during the development section depend on your opening statement.

TRACK 02   TRACK 03
           Slow Demo

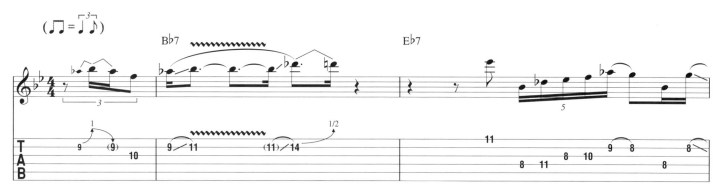

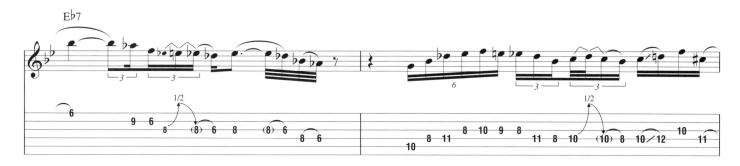

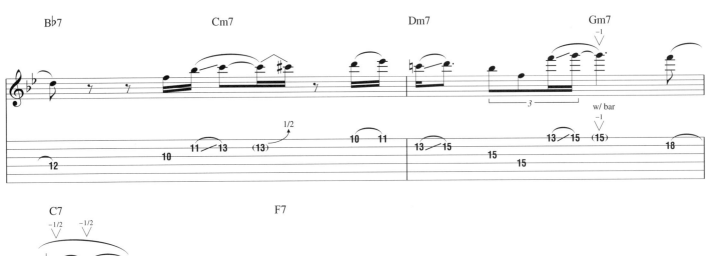

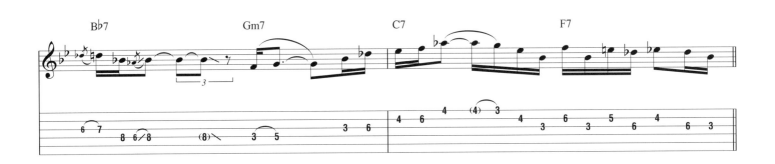

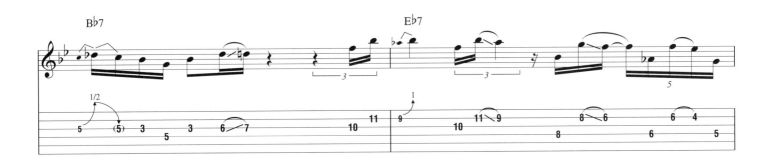

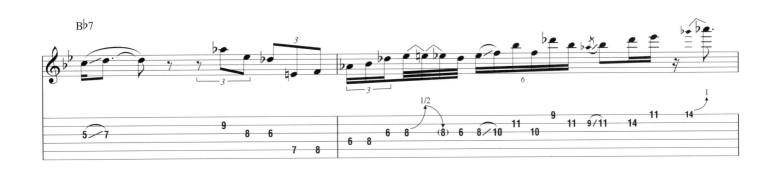

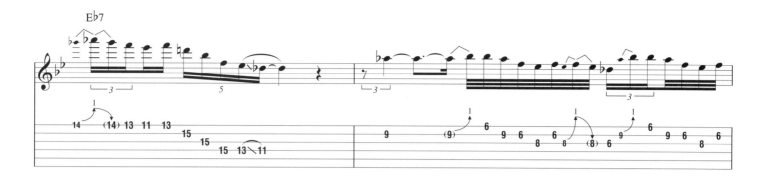

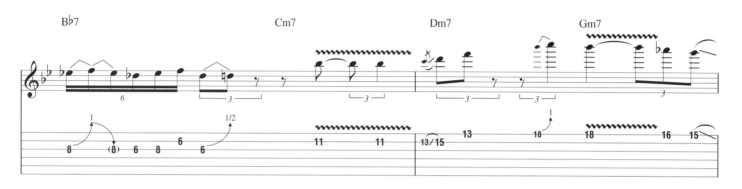

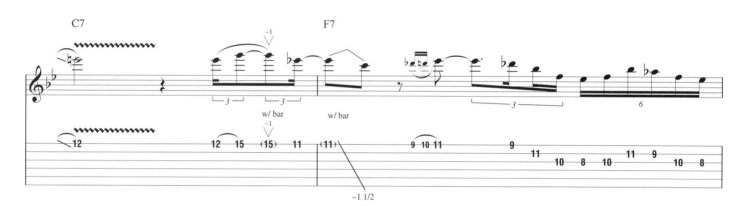

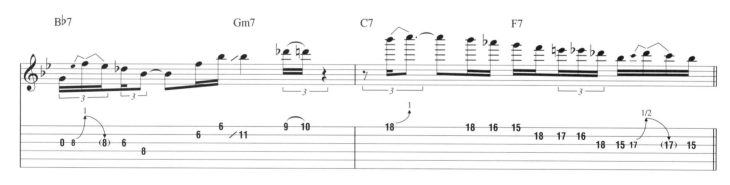

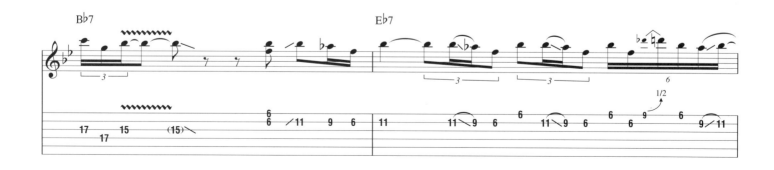

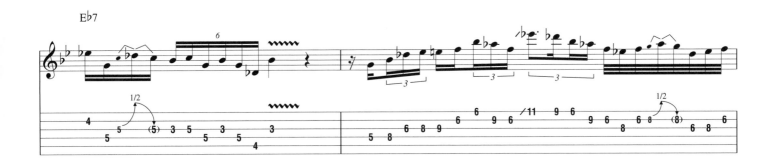

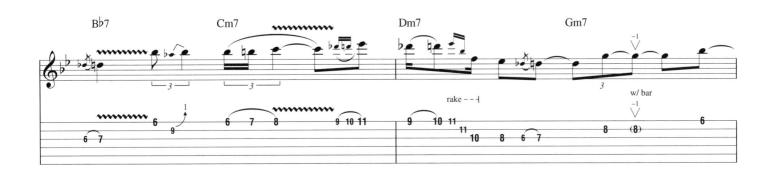

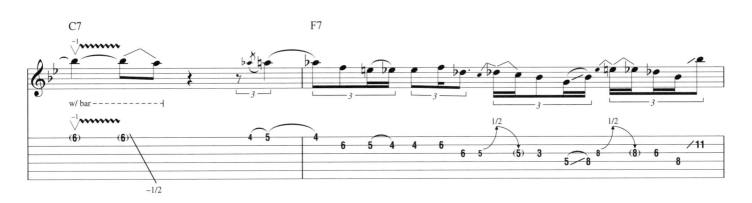

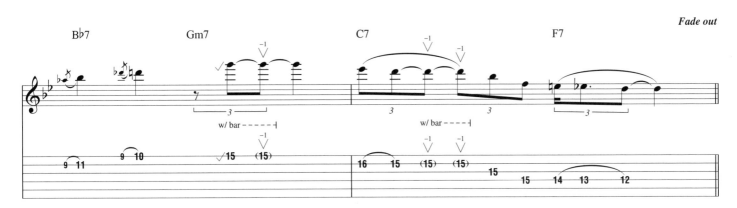

9

As for any good storyteller, it's important for you to know what you want to say before you say it. It's also much easier to develop a solo when you know exactly where you're going. Once you've established your "feeling tone" and harmonic center, the rest of the solo is simply following your story outline.

Here's another example of an opening statement with a different feeling tone for the same song. This one is aggressive.

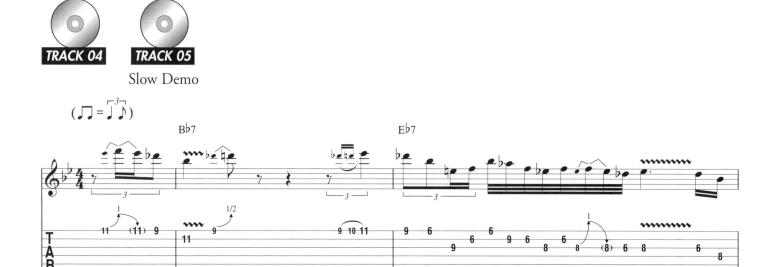

Slow Demo

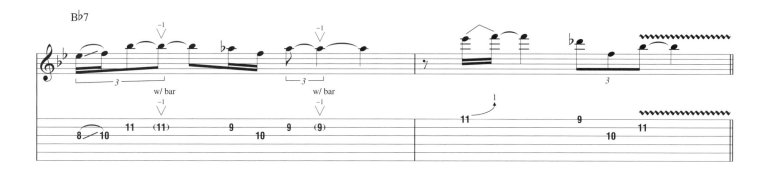

The beautiful thing about music is that it can be different every time you play it, and it's important to be able to apply different emotions to a solo. Both examples work for the song, and you can pick your own feeling tone based on how you feel in the moment when you're playing.

Now, here's the backing track for "Buzz's Blues" so you can practice on your own. Try different feeling tones for yourself, and see which ones feel the best for you. When you solo on your own, select a harmonic home base—a key that works for you for the song. It's usually obvious: If the song is an E minor blues, your harmonic center will, of course, be E minor. If the song is in C major, the harmonic center will be C major. The practice track for "Buzz's Blues" happens to be in the key of B♭ major.

TRACK 06

THE STORY, PART II

Development

The second section of a solo is the development section. This is where you create tension and explore the full range of your feeling tone. Once you've made your opening statement, you know your basic style and your harmonic home base, but as in any good story, you need conflict and tension. Tension is the most important part of this section—it's how you keep the listener's attention.

Tension can be created in three ways.

- Harmonic variation
- Rhythmic variation
- Dynamic variation

We'll take a look at each of these in a moment, but first let's talk a little bit more about feeling tones.

VARYING THE FEELING TONE

In, for example, a "cocky" feeling tone solo, I would make bold and aggressive statements, leave some space between phrases, and build the development section with some very fast scale motion. I'd also choose a climactic ending, rather than an ending that sounds like a transition into something else. Here is an example of this cocky approach to a solo.

"Little Sister"

TRACK 07   TRACK 08
Slow Demo

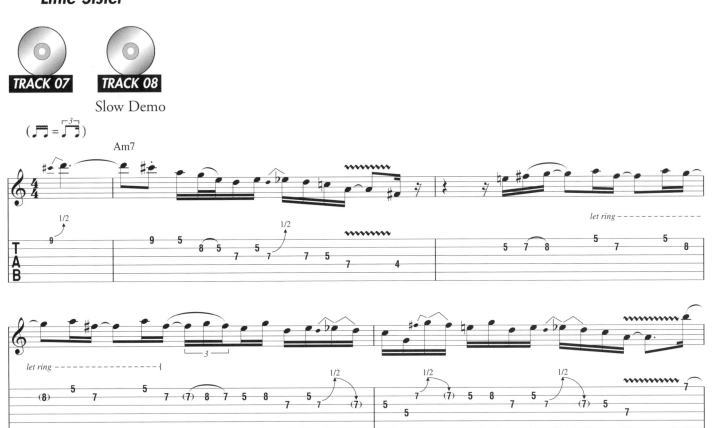

Em7

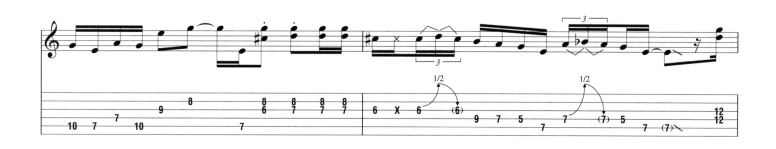

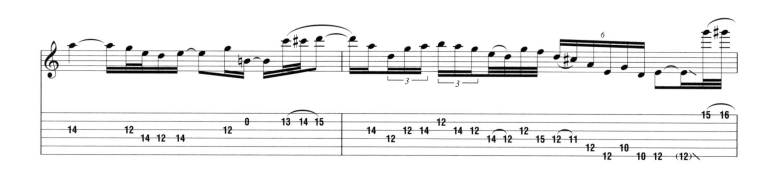

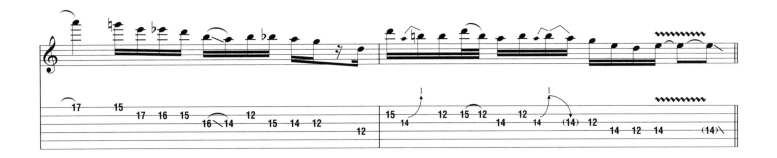

D

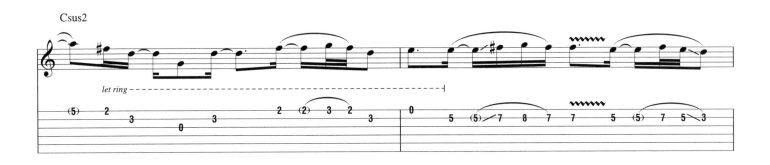

Csus2

D

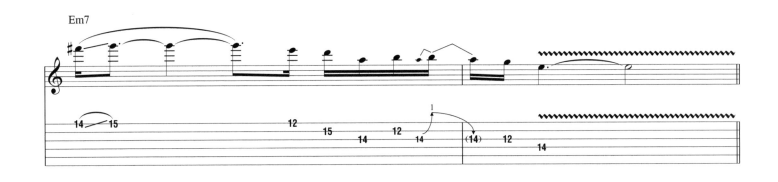

Em7

In a "mysterious" feeling tone solo, I would make the opening statement less aggressive and more evocative or teasing. In the development section, I would choose notes that are more dissonant (in other words "clashing," or not part of the chord or a scale that would work over the chord), and include a lot of half steps and big interval jumps. The ending would be less aggressive than the previous one and would sound more like a transition. Note that the first 16 bars are the intro; the solo begins in measure 17, just after the double bar.

"Party Shoes"

Slow Demo

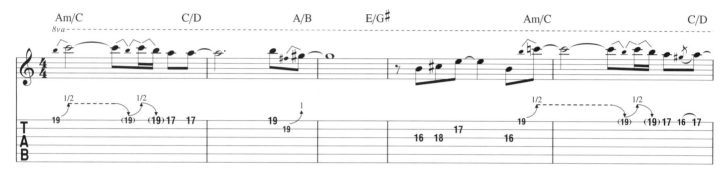

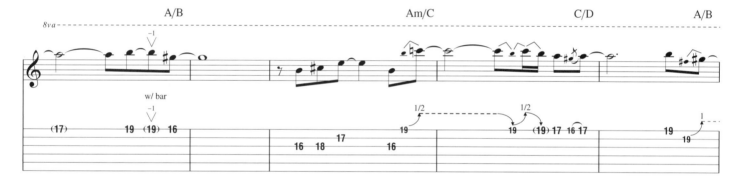

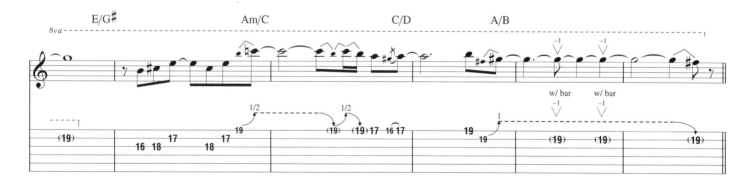

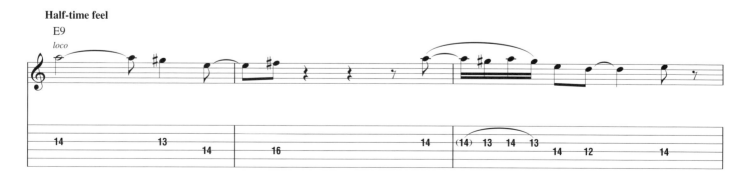

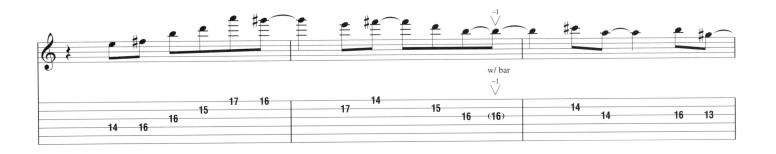

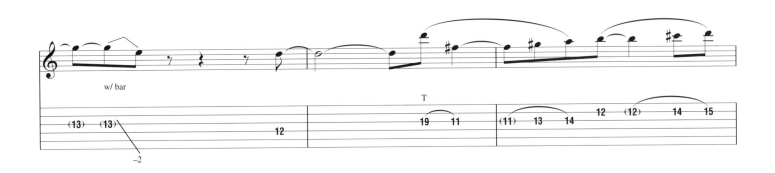

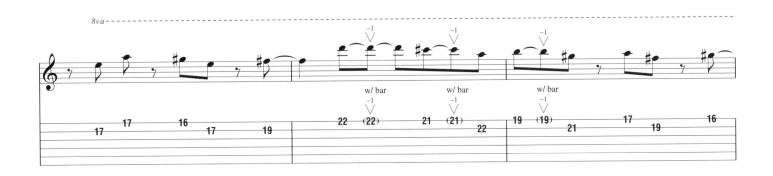

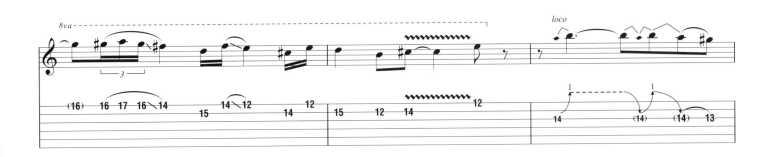

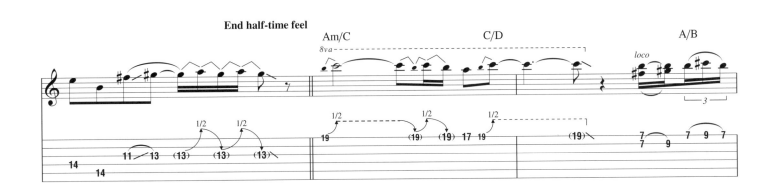

15

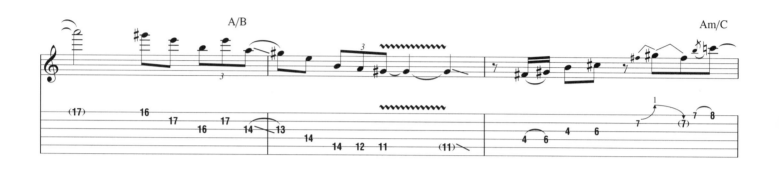

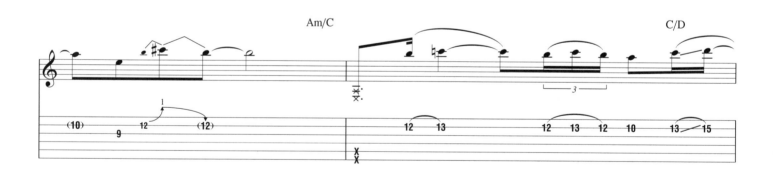

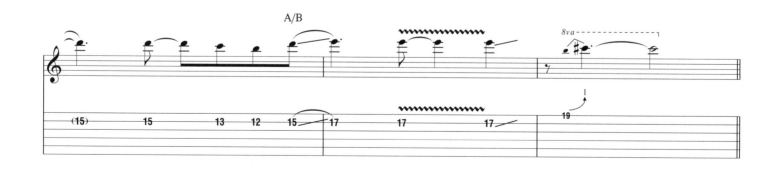

Here are the backing tracks for the above songs. As you play along to them, try to incorporate some of the above ideas and experiment with different feeling tones.

"Little Sister" Practice Track

"Party Shoes" Practice Track

HARMONIC VARIATION

In the development section, it's very effective to change the harmonic "center" in order to create tension. This doesn't necessarily mean that you change keys—only that you *think* in a different harmony, regardless of what notes the bass player plays or what the chords from the keyboard happen to be. This technique creates a tension—a subtle dissonance in the midst of the rest of the band—that can be very effective. Here's an example of this "transposed thinking" in "Little Sister."

Slow Demo

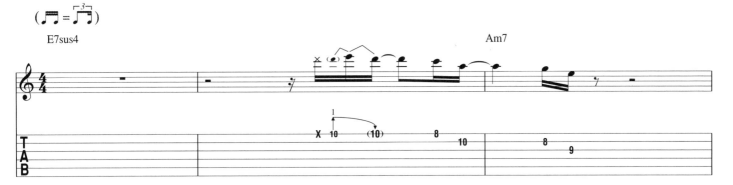

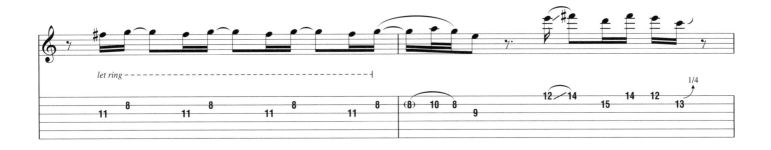

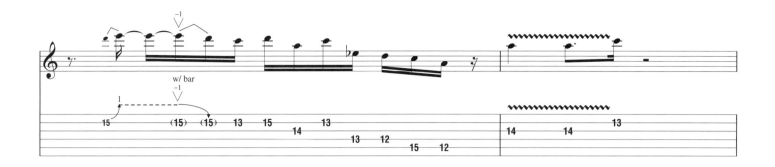

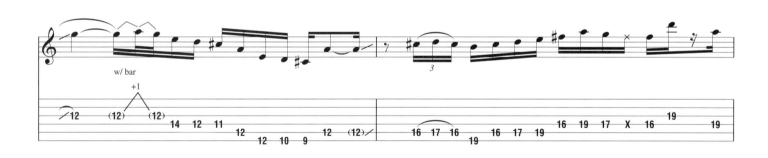

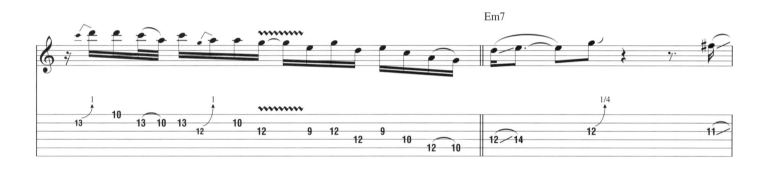

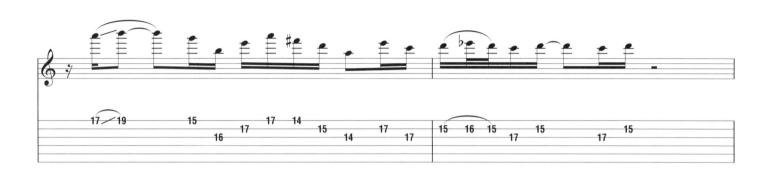

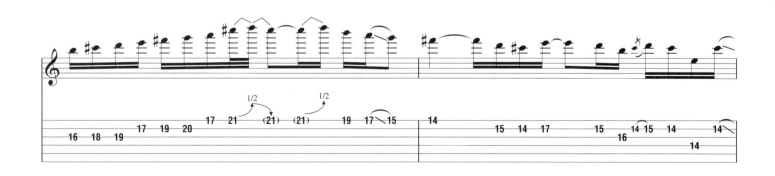

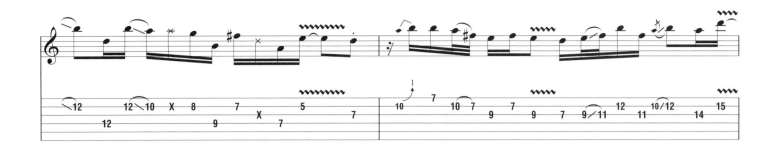

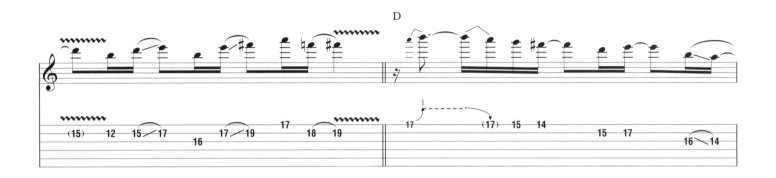

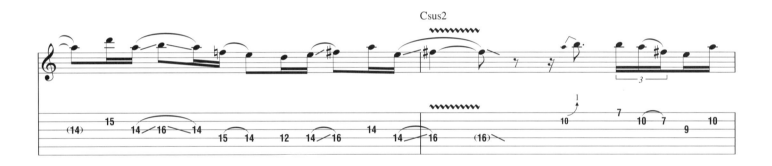

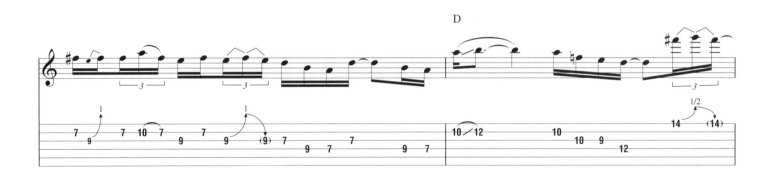

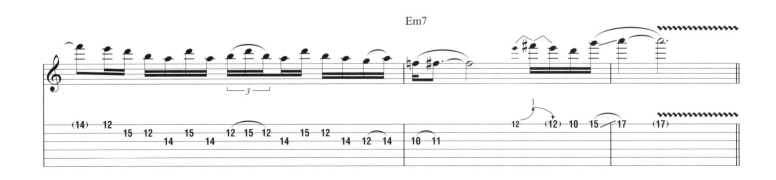

The band here is playing over an Am7 for eight measures (beginning in measure 3, the bar just after the solo makes its entrance), but just after that in the middle/development section, it goes to Em. For that section, I started "thinking" in terms of B minor. It's a very useful trick to use to create tension leading up to the climax of a solo.

Here is a chart you can use to find a good "thinking" key—in other words, the key you will be thinking in as opposed to the actual key of the song.

Actual Harmony	"Thinking" Options
E	B minor: Go up a 5th and think in that minor key. G# minor blues: Go up a major 3rd and think in that minor key (blues scale).
E7	B minor blues: Go up a 5th and think in that minor key (blues scale). A major: Go up a 4th and think in that major key. D major: Go down a whole step and think in that major key.
Em	B minor blues: Go up a 5th and think in that minor key (blues scale). C major: Go down a major 3rd and think in that major key.

When the song is in a different key, simply use the intervals given in the chart above to find your "thinking" harmony.

"Break Down These Walls"

Here are two more examples of transposed thinking.

Listen to bar 9 of the solo. That's the point at which I started to think more in A minor. Can you hear how suddenly the solo started to have more tension? I also started playing some very fast scale motion. The combination of those two elements in the development section adds to the tension in the solo.

TRACK 15   TRACK 16
            Slow Demo

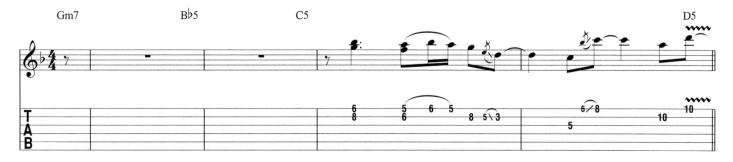

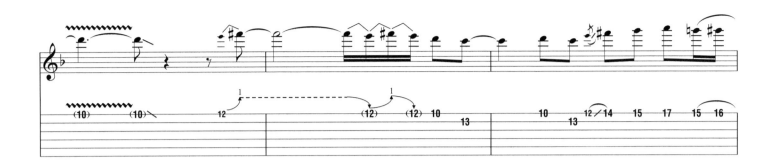

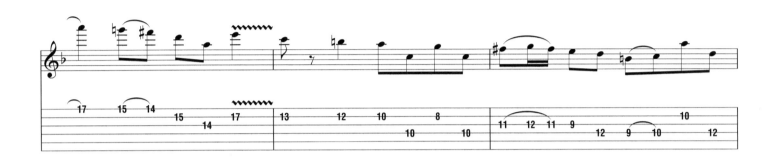

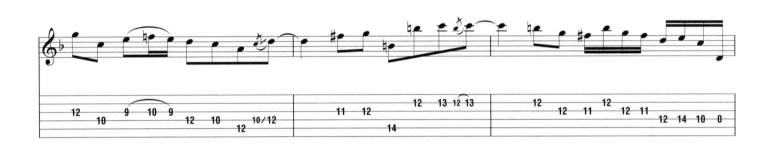

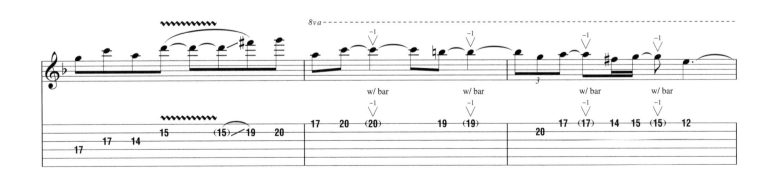

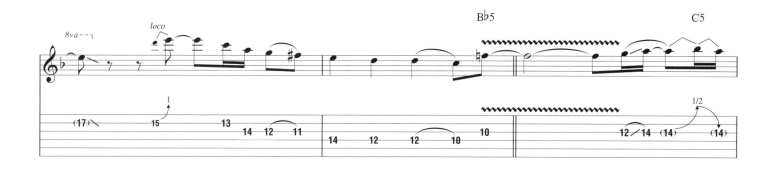

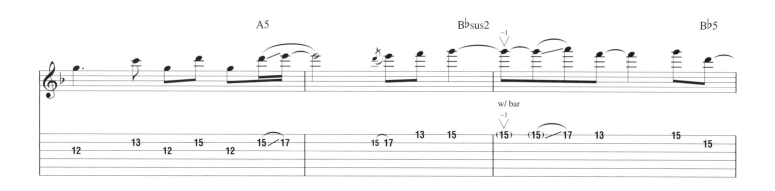

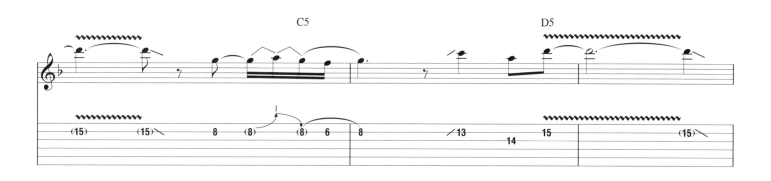

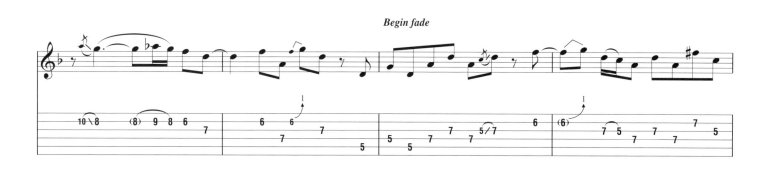

In this solo, I started thinking largely in A minor right away and continued for 11 measures. This is another way to get the listener's attention. After this, I started to build the tension instead by getting bluesier; in the two bars right before the chord change to B♭5 in measure 20, I played a long, fast scale pattern leading up to the change and held the high note over that change. That can be very effective as a climax to a solo.

TRACK 17   TRACK 18

Slow Demo

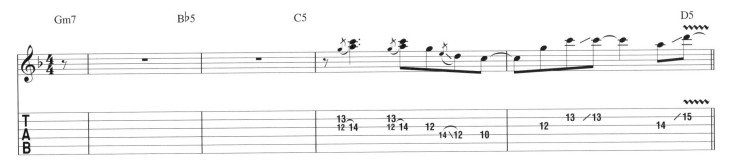

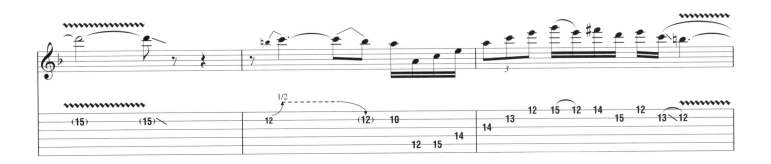

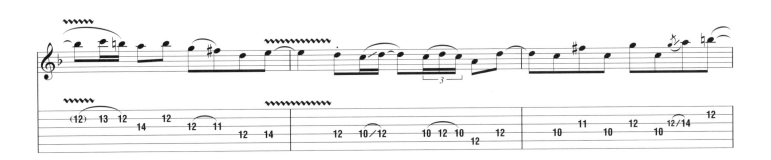

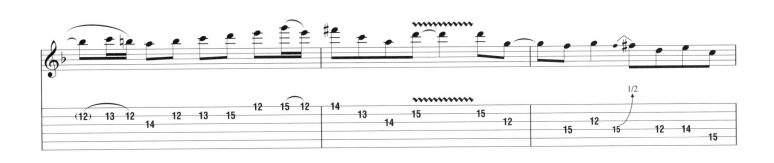

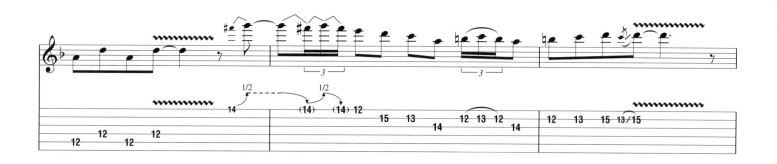

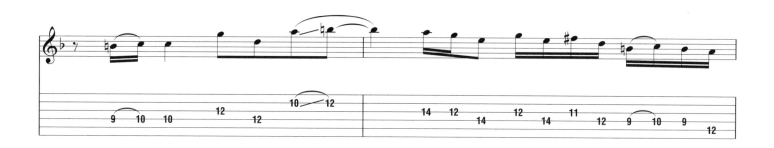

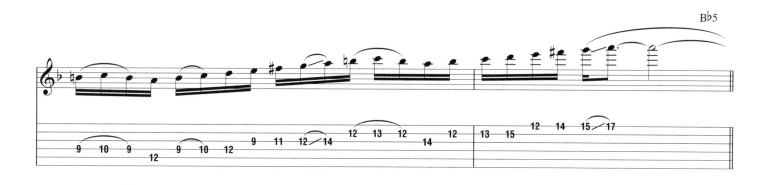

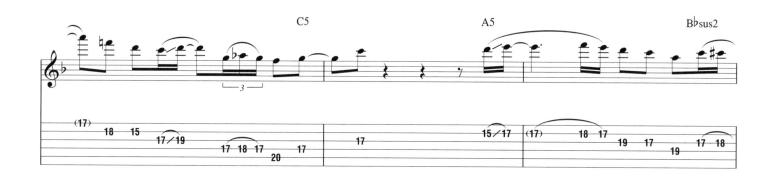

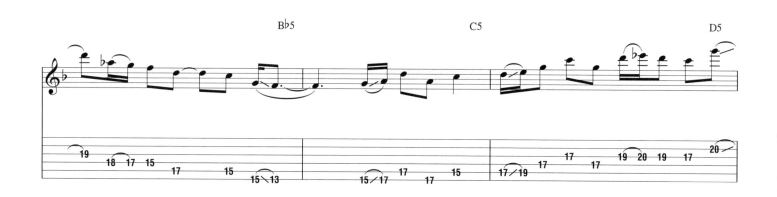

24

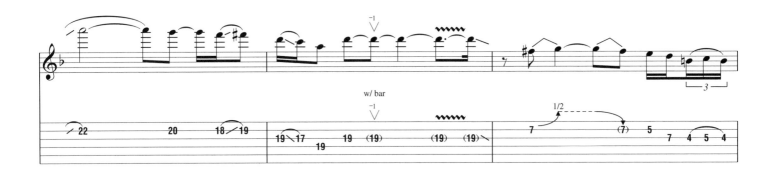

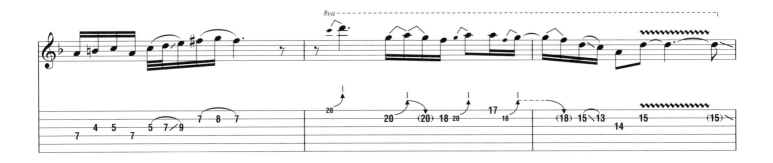

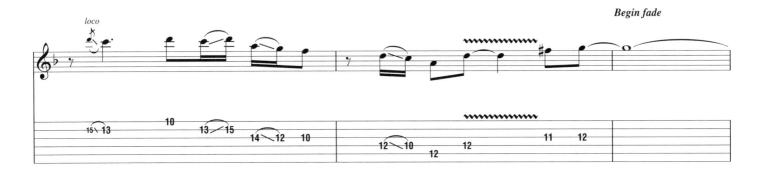

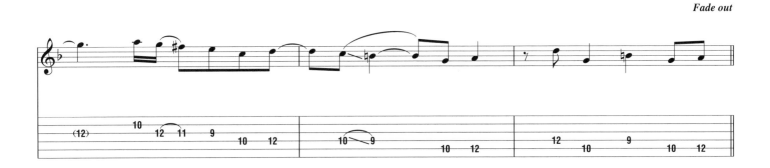

Here's a backing track so you can practice to "Break Down These Walls."

Try thinking in alternate keys whenever you solo. You'll be amazed at how interesting your solos can sound!

25

RHYTHMIC VARIATION

Miles Davis said that rhythm is more important than notes, and I believe that's true. The development section is where you can start to create tension by mixing up the rhythmic patterns.

"Party Shoes"

You start the solo with an opening statement, but now you can start to engage the listener by adding more notes and changing the rhythmic patterns. Here are two examples of a solo where the pitches are similar, but the rhythms are varied. In the first, the solo begins in measure 16, just before the double bar.

Slow Demo

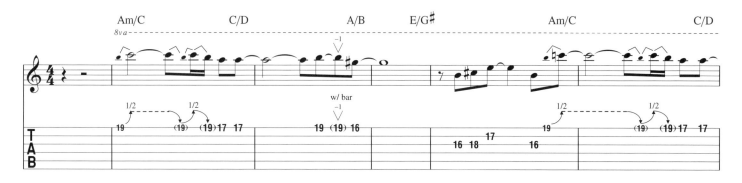

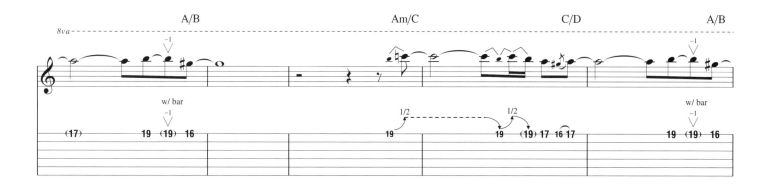

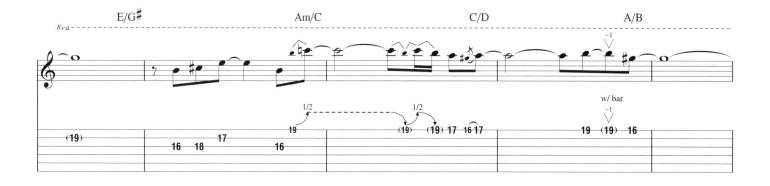

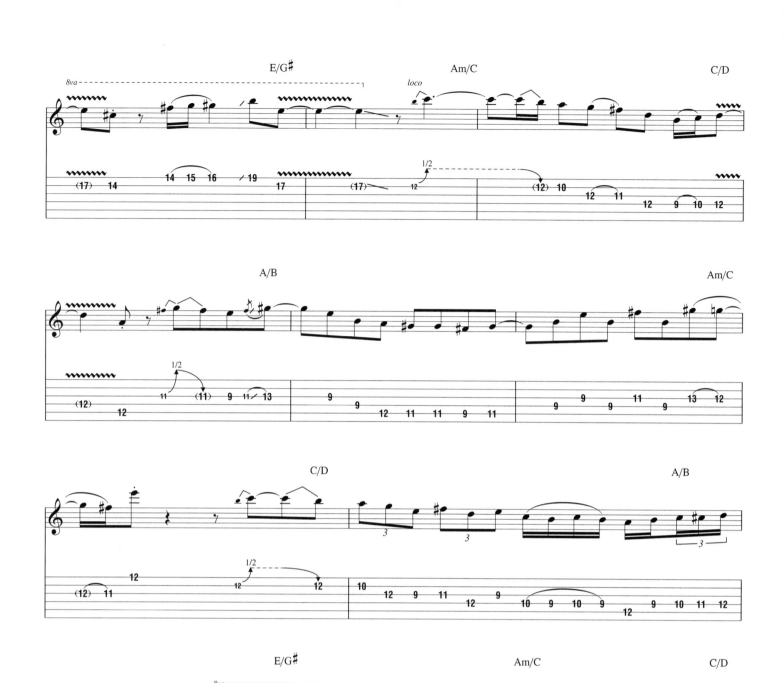

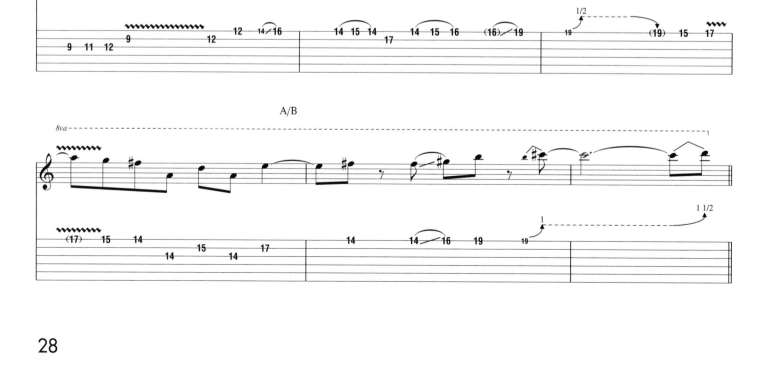

In this example, the solo begins in measure 17, at the half-time feel just after the double bar.

These are good examples of the importance of rhythmic variation in your solo. Robben Ford is an excellent model of a soloist who uses a lot of rhythmic variation. His solos are always exciting and interesting.

DYNAMIC VARIATION

There's an old joke about when a guitar player was asked about his dynamics, he responded by asking, "What do you mean 'dynamics'? I'm playing as loud as I can!" There's a lot of truth in that joke. Many guitarists think "dynamics" means "playing as loud as you can," but the best solos—and the best music in general—include a wide range of dynamic potential.

Larry Carlton is a good example of a player who uses dynamics well. His solos are always interesting and effective because he captures our attention with his use of dynamics. For instance, if the full range of dynamic potential is between "1" and "10," you should try to use everything from "2" to "9" in your solos. That doesn't necessarily mean that you should always start at "2" and end up at "10." Sometimes, you'll want to start out loud, drop down for a dramatic effect, and then build the volume back up again. Whichever approach you choose, you need to use all of the tension-creating devices available to you. That's your job as a soloist.

THREE DIFFERENT APPROACHES TO THE SAME SONG

The following three tracks are different approaches to the same song. Try playing them back-to-back. It's a great illustration of how the possibilities in soloing are endless. Notice how each solo has a beginning, a development section, and an ending. In each development section, you can increase the tension in the story by introducing harmonic, rhythmic, and dynamic variations.

"Dinwiddie" from New Full Moon

Slow Demo

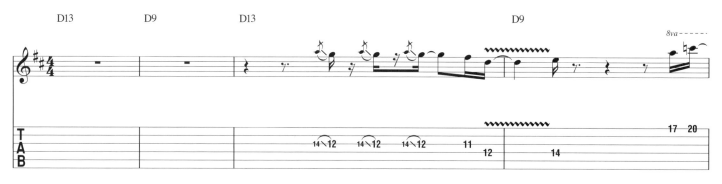

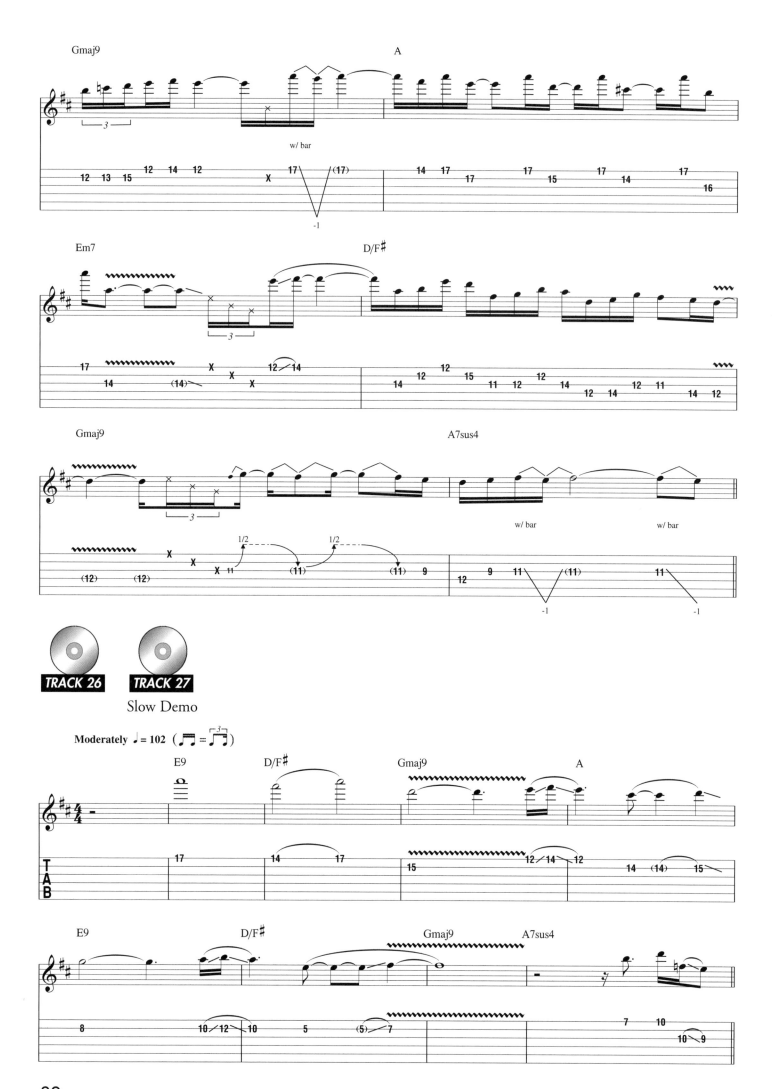

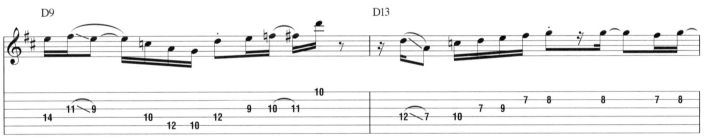

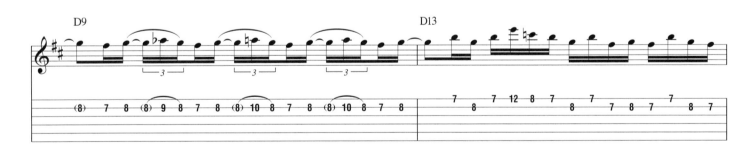

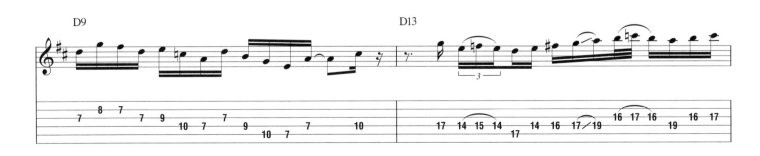

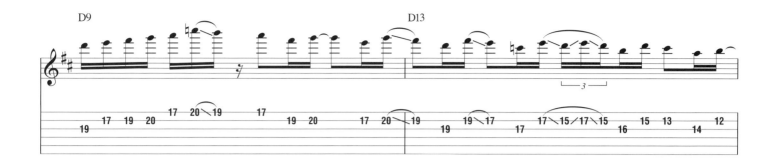

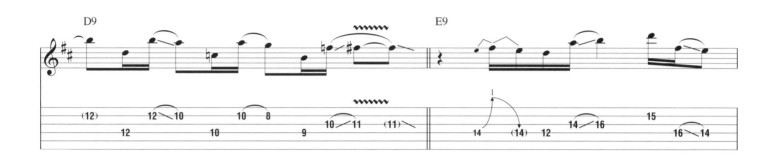

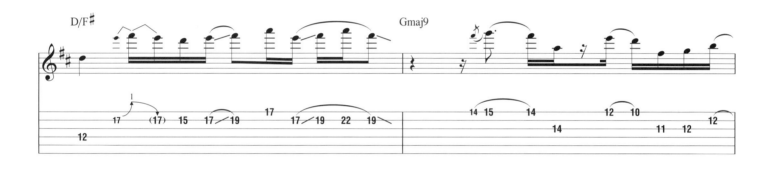

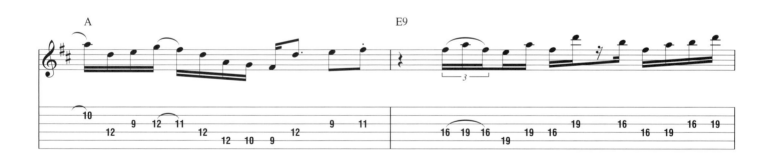

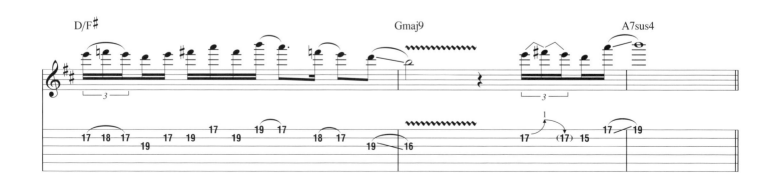

TRACK 28   TRACK 29
Slow Demo

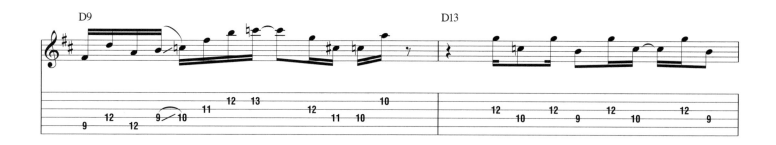

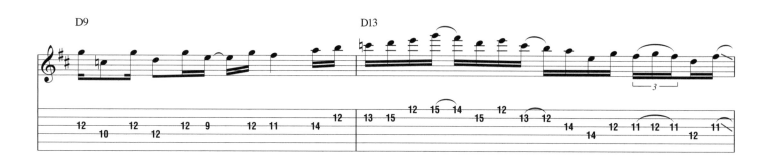

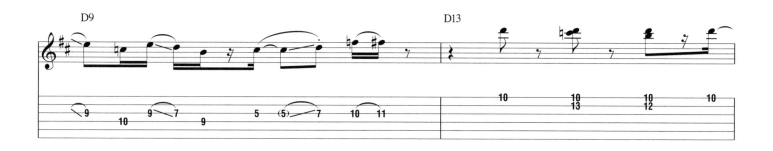

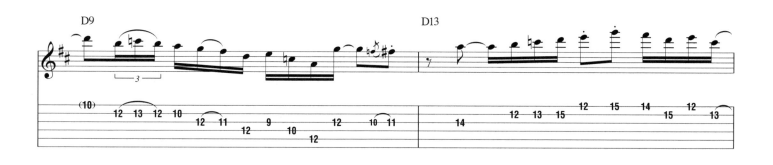

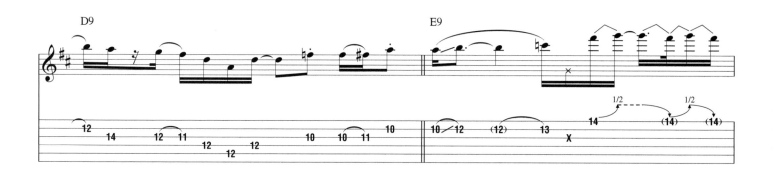

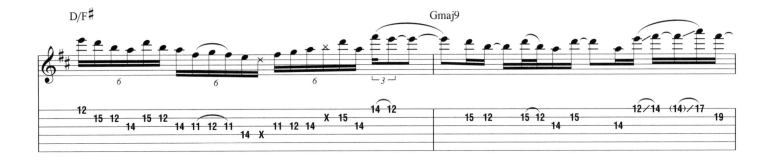

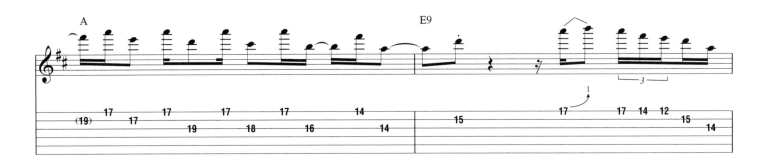

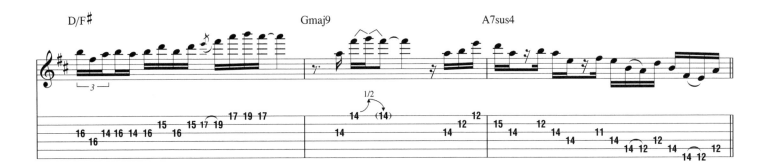

After listening to the examples, it's easy to hear how each solo has the same building blocks, but there are variations among them. Here's a "Dinwiddie" backing track for practice.

TRACK 30

THE STORY, PART III

The Ending

How you end your solo is at least as important as how you handle the beginning and middle sections. For your listeners, it's the last thing they hear and, as a result, usually the last thing they remember. It's often the high point or climax of your story, but not always. Most of the time you arrive at your peak just before the end of the solo, and the last phrase serves as a connection back to the rest of the song.

The ending should be a resolution of the conflict and tension you created in the body of the solo using your harmonic, rhythmic, and dynamic variations. It can be very effective to return to the simple theme or melody you created in the opening statement.

The ending leads back into the song, so if the song gets louder after the solo, you should make the ending your climax. If the song gets softer, you'll need to make your song climax slightly earlier, and make the last few bars a transition back into the song by getting gradually simpler and quieter.

Listen to these two different solos from "Little Sister" and pay attention to the way in which each ends.

This one is a good example of a "climax" ending.

TRACK 31   **TRACK 32**

Slow Demo

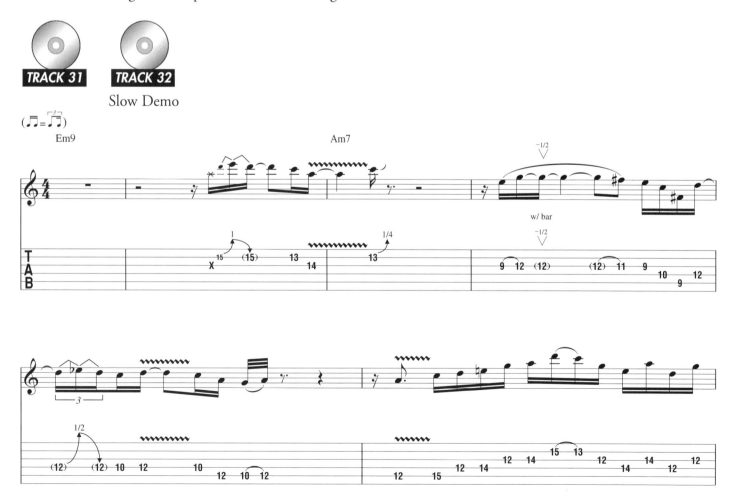

D

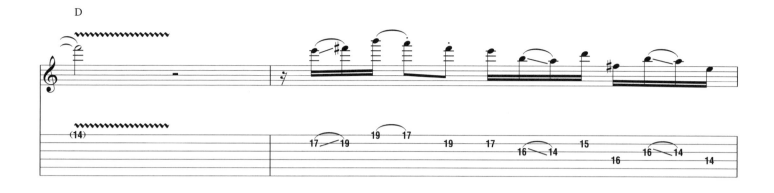

Csus2

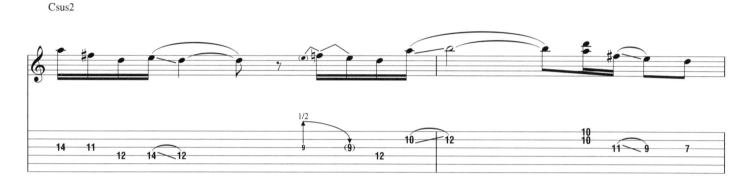

D

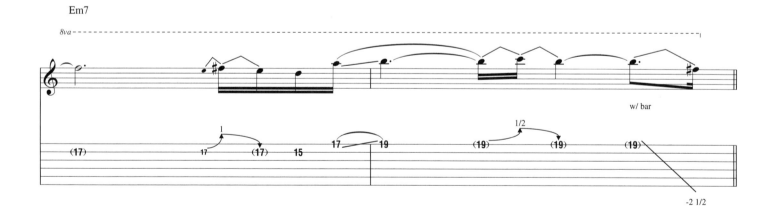

Em7

Now, compare that with the solo that begins on page 11, which is a perfect example of a "transition" ending. Notice the differences, particularly in where the high points fall.

ADDITIONAL TOPICS AND TECHNIQUES

VIBRATO

The left-hand vibrato or "shake" is a basic technique that is essential for the blues/rock soloist. Practice resting the largest knuckle joint of the 1st finger of your left hand on the neck, with your 2nd finger on a string, and gently rock your left hand, using the knuckle joint as a pivot point. Here's an example of how it should sound.

BENDS

String-bending is an incredibly useful tool to add passion and expression to your solos. Here are three different bends that I use all the time.

Half Step Bend

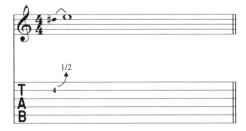

Whole Step Bend

TRACK 35

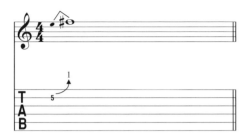

Minor 3rd Bend

TRACK 36

Practice each of these bends, making sure that the note you bend up to is solidly in tune.

SLIDES

Sliding between notes gives a different effect than bending. Here are three different slides that I use.

Half Step Slide

TRACK 37

Whole Step Slide

Minor 3rd Slide

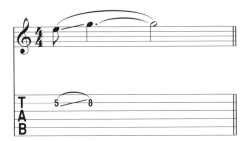

HAMMER-ONS AND PULL-OFFS

These are techniques that I use all the time. They give a nice variation to your phrasing. Below are some minor 3rd hammer-ons combined with pull-offs.

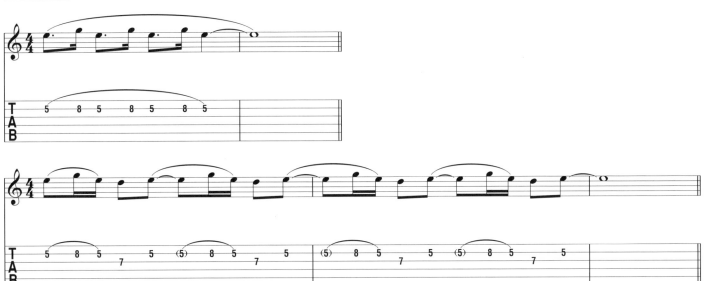

SAMPLE EXERCISES

from *Warm-Ups and Exercises for the Blues/Rock Guitarist*

MAJOR ARPEGGIO

TRACK 41

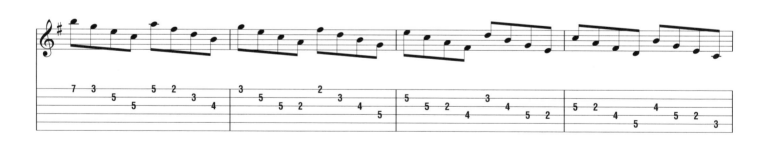

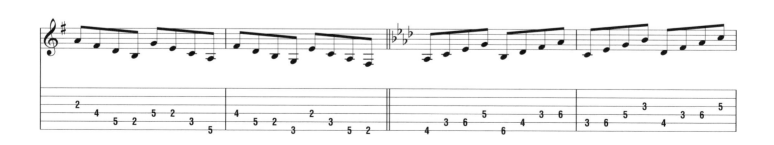

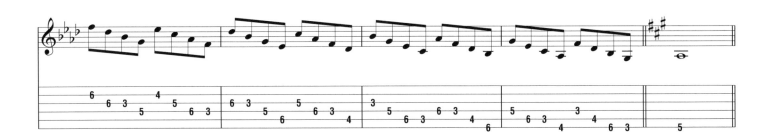

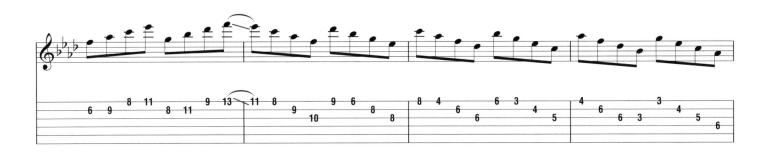

SIXTHS IN A MAJOR SCALE PATTERN

TRACK 42

DIMINISHED ARPEGGIO IN AN UPWARD PATTERN

TRACK 43

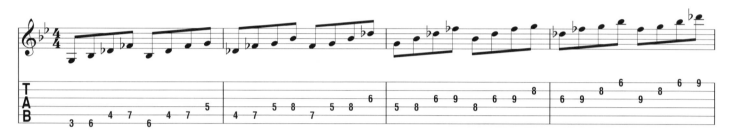

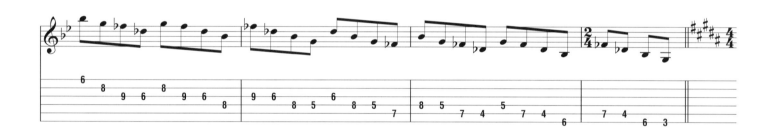

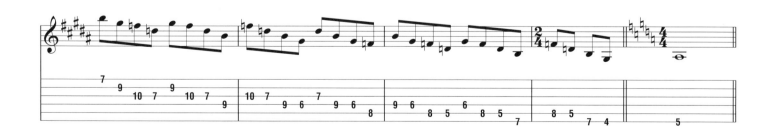

BUZZ FEITEN

A Selected Discography

BUZZ'S LATEST RELEASES

Buzz Feiten & The New Full Moon
Full Moon Live, Full Moon (the original studio recording re-released)
Buzz Feiten—*Whirlies*
Buzz Feiten & The Whirlies—*Live at the Baked Potato: Hollywood 6-4-99*

A SELECTION OF BUZZ'S OTHER RECORDINGS

Gregg Allman—*Laid Back*
George Benson—*George Benson Collection*
Stephen Bishop—*Red Cab to Manhattan*
The Paul Butterfield Blues Band—*Keep on Moving*
Felix Cavaliere—*Destiny*
Chicago—*Chicago 18*
Gene Clark—*No Other*
Commander Cody & The Lost…—*Flying Dreams*
Randy Crawford—*Windsong*
Bob Dylan—*New Morning*
Aretha Franklin—*Spirit in the Dark; One Lord, One Faith, One Baptism*
Michael Franks—*Blue Pacific*
Footlose—*Original Soundtrack*
Free Creek—*Summit Meeting*
Full Moon—*Full Moon*
Stefan Grossman—*Perspective*
Hall & Oates—*Change of Season*
Stuart Hamm—*Kings of Sleep, Urge*
Fareed Haque—*Sacred Addicition*
Rickie Lee Jones—*Rickie Lee Jones, Pirates, Flying Cowboys*
Bobby King & Terry Evans—*Rhythm, Blues Soul & Grooves*
Dave Koz—*Dave Koz, Lucky Man*
Labelle—*Pressure Cookin'*
Neil Larsen—*Jungle Fever, High Gear*
Larsen-Feiten Band—*Larsen-Feiten Band, Full Moon*
Kenny Loggins—*Vox Humana*
Jeff Lorber—*Private Passion, Worth Waiting For*

Love—*Reel to Real*

Don McLean—*Don McLean*

Larry John McNally—*Fade to Black*

Bette Midler—*Experience the Divine*

Randy Newman—*Land of Dreams*

The Young Rascals—*Peaceful World, Island of Real*

David Sanborn—*Taking Off, Voyeur*

Boz Scaggs—*Other Roads*

Tom Scott—*Street Beat*

Ben Sidran—*Cat and the Hat*

Edwin Starr—*Stronger Than You Think I Am*

Syreeta—*Syreeta*

Livingston Taylor—*Over the Rainbow*

Jennifer Warnes—*Shot Through the Heart*

Dave Weckl—*Rhythm of the Soul, Synergy*

Stevie Wonder—*Music of My Mind, Talking Book, Songs in the Key of Life*